Riding to the Rescue!

Ambulances

B.J. Best

Cavendish
Square
New York

Published in 2018 by Cavendish Square Publishing, LLC
243 5th Avenue, Suite 136, New York, NY 10016

Copyright © 2018 by Cavendish Square Publishing, LLC

First Edition

Website: cavendishsq.com

This publication represents the opinions and views of the author based on his or her personal experience, knowledge, and research. The information in this book serves as a general guide only. The author and publisher have used their best efforts in preparing this book and disclaim liability rising directly or indirectly from the use and application of this book.

CPSIA Compliance Information: Batch #CS17CSQ

All websites were available and accurate when this book was sent to press.

Library of Congress Cataloging-in-Publication Data

Names: Best, B. J., 1976- author.
Title: Ambulances / B.J. Best.
Description: New York : Cavendish Square Publishing, 2018. | Series: Riding to the rescue! | Includes index.
Identifiers: LCCN 2016047275 (print) | LCCN 2016048349 (ebook) | ISBN 9781502625717 (pbk.) | ISBN 9781502625533 (6 pack) | ISBN 9781502625656 (library bound) | ISBN 9781502625595 (E-book)
Subjects: LCSH: Ambulances--Juvenile literature.
Classification: LCC TL235.8 .B47 2017 (print) | LCC TL235.8 (ebook) | DDC 629.222/34--dc23
LC record available at https://lccn.loc.gov/2016047275

The photographs in this book are used by permission and through the courtesy of:
Cover Venturelli Luca/Shutterstock; p. 5 Leonardo Patrizi/Getty Images Entertainment/Getty Images; p. 7 Air Images/Shutterstock; p. 9 Caiaimage/Paul Bradbury/Getty Images Entertainment/Getty Images; p. 11 Thinkstock Images/Getty Images Entertainment/Getty Images; p. 13 Tyler Olson/Shutterstock; p. 15 michaeljung/Shutterstock; p. 19 Paul Burns/Getty Images Entertainment/Getty Images; p. 21 Edward McCain/Getty Images Entertainment/Getty Images.

Printed in the United States of America

Contents

There is a loud siren.

There are bright lights.

An ambulance is coming
to the rescue!

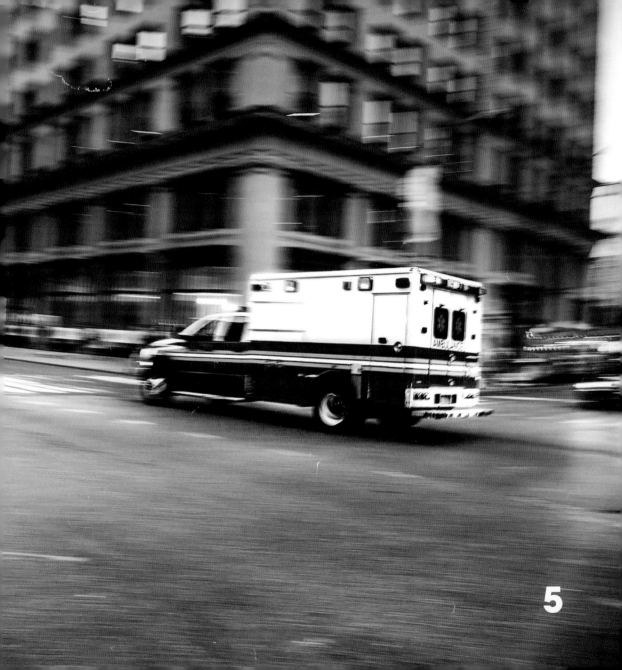

5

Ambulances help people who are very sick.

They help people who are very hurt.

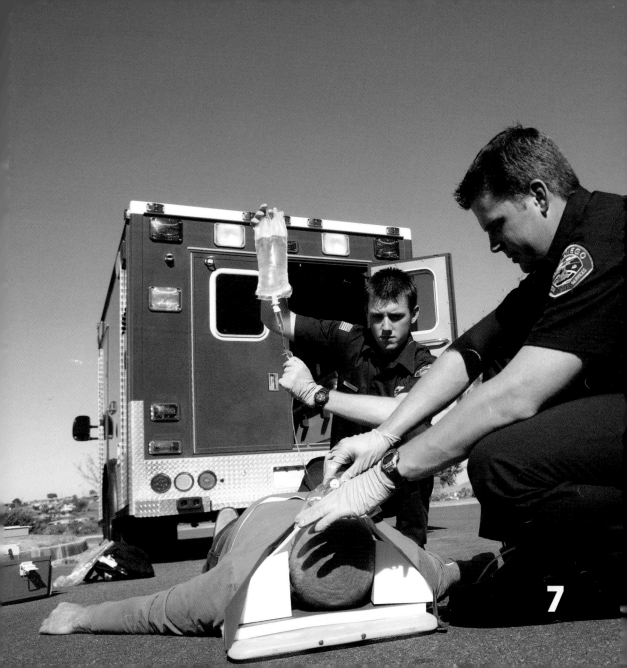

People who work in ambulances are called **EMTs**.

They are Emergency Medical **Technicians**.

9

The EMTs get a call on
the radio.

Someone is **injured**!

The ambulance drives fast.

11

The EMTs do not waste time.

The EMTs help the **patient**.

The patient often needs to go to the hospital.

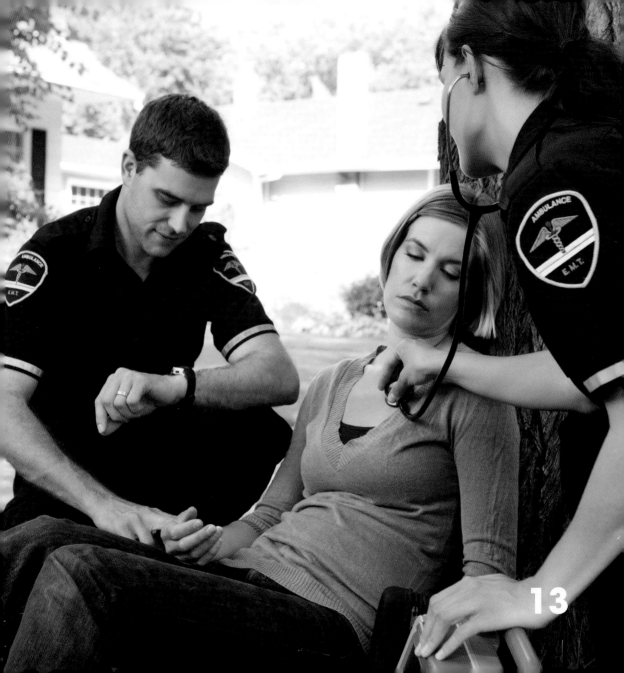

13

A patient rides in the back.

A patient rides on a bed.

It is called a **gurney**.

15

The EMTs have many tools in the back.

It is like a small hospital inside.

The ambulance arrives at the hospital.

Nurses and doctors will care for the patient.

AMBULANCE ENTRANCE ONLY

PARAMEDIC
UNIT

19

The ambulance gets another call.

It drives away to help.

EMTs save lives!

21

New Words

EMTs (E-M-TEES) People who work in an ambulance.

gurney (GER-nee) A bed with wheels.

injured (IN-jerd) Hurt or sick.

patient (PAY-shent) A person getting medical care.

technicians (teck-NIH-shuns) People with skills.

Index

About the Author

B.J. Best lives in Wisconsin with his wife and son. He has written many other books for children. He has never ridden in an ambulance.

About BOOKWORMS

Bookworms help independent readers gain reading confidence through high-frequency words, simple sentences, and strong picture/text support. Each book explores a concept that helps children relate what they read to the world they live in.